knit along with

along with

DEBBIE MACOMBER

Hannah's List

LEISURE ARTS, INC.
Little Rock, Arkansas

EDITORIAL STAFF
Editor-in-Chief: Susan White Sullivan
Knit and Crochet Publications Director: Debra Nettles
Special Projects Director: Susan Frantz Wiles
Senior Prepress Director: Mark Hawkins
Art Publications Director: Rhonda Shelby
Technical Editor: Cathy Hardy
Contributing Editors: Linda Daley, Sarah J. Green, and Lois J. Long
Editorial Writer: Susan McManus Johnson
Art Category Manager: Lora Puls
Graphic Artists: Dayle Carozza and Amy Temple
Production Artist: Janie Wright
Imaging Technicians: Brian Hall, Stephanie Johnson, and Mark R. Potter
Photography Manager: Katherine Laughlin
Contributing Photographers: Jason Masters and Ken West
Contributing Photostylists: Cora Brown and Christy Myers
Publishing Systems Administrator: Becky Riddle
Publishing Systems Assistants: Clint Hanson

BUSINESS STAFF
Vice President and Chief Operations Officer: Tom Siebenmorgen
Director of Finance and Administration: Laticia Mull Dittrich
Vice President, Sales and Marketing: Pam Stebbins
National Accounts Director: Martha Adams
Sales and Services Director: Margaret Reinhold
Information Technology Director: Hermine Linz
Controller: Francis Caple
Vice President, Operations: Jim Dittrich
Comptroller, Operations: Rob Thieme
Retail Customer Service Manager: Stan Raynor
Print Production Manager: Fred F. Pruss

ISBN-13: 978-1-60900-041-7

10 9 8 7 6 5 4 3 2 1

table of CONTENTS

debbie MACOMBER

photo by Nina Subin

Dear Friends,

Is there anything more inviting than the huge range of colors and fibers you find in a yarn shop? It boggles the mind! Even so, I always know who in my family needs a scarf, sweater, or afghan. I don't think it's a coincidence that a visit to a yarn shop always brings loved ones to mind.

In my latest Blossom Street story, *Hannah's List*, knitting helps a tenderhearted young woman reach out to a friend who is ill. For a young widower, a remembered gift of knitting reminds him that there are many different ways of showing love. Knitting also becomes an expression of concern for an elderly neighbor, as well as preparation for a happy event.

In my own life, it's no secret that I have a real passion for collecting yarn—I always want to have plenty available to make gifts for my eight wonderful grandkids! My yarn stash has been known to get a little—okay, a lot—out of hand. If you find that keeping your knitting organized is a bit of a challenge, you may be interested in the Knit Along with Debbie Macomber Collection at TheLeisureBoutique.com. There are several totes and a journal to keep track of your projects and supplies. You'll also find patterns, notions, and a CD of printable note cards.

Another thing that's important to me is helping those in need, so I've donated the proceeds from sales of my Leisure Arts Knit Along books and the knitter's product line to my favorite charities, including Warm Up America! and World Vison. On page 41, you'll find two blocks to knit for your own community charity efforts.

Of course, there's something else about knitting that makes me happy—knowing that so many good people love it as much as I do! This book's for you!

Debbie

a word from
LEISURE ARTS
and MIRA books

LOOK FOR DEBBIE'S HEARTWARMING STORIES AT BOOKSTORES
EVERYWHERE, AND COLLECT ALL TEN OF HER KNITTING PUBLICATIONS!

knit along with
DEBBIE MACOMBER

Read The Books that Inspired the Projects

Cedar Cove Series

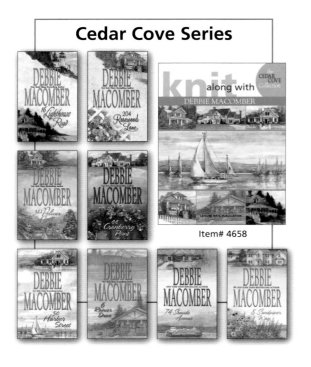

Item# 4658

Inspired by Debbie's popular Blossom Street and Cedar Cove book series, the *Knit Along with Debbie Macomber* companion books are a treasure trove of patterns to knit! And have you discovered the classic patterns in *Debbie's Favorites* or the thoughtful designs in *Friendship Shawls*? Take time to indulge yourself with Debbie's warm and memorable tales; then treat yourself to a little creativity from Leisure Arts!

Other Debbie Macomber Publications

Item# 4692

Item# 4504

Item# 4803

LEISURE ARTS
the art of everyday living

To find out more about Debbie Macomber, visit
www.debbiemacomber.com or www.mirabooks.com.

For information about these and other Leisure Arts
publications, call 1.800.526.5111 or visit www.leisurearts.com.

meet the CHARACTERS
from *hannah's list*

Michael Everett

Hannah taught me that, when you love someone, you need to show that love each and every day. A year ago today I lost her, my beautiful thirty-six-year-old wife. Can you imagine my surprise when Hannah's brother, Ritchie, gave me an envelope today and said, "Hannah asked me to give you this after she'd been gone a year."

In all these months Ritchie had never let on that he had this letter in his possession. I don't know how long I stared at the letter before I found the courage to open it.

My darling Michael,

I know this letter will come as a shock to you and I apologize for that. It's been a year now and I imagine it's been a difficult one for you. I have one final request of you, and I hope you will honor it. I want you to marry again. I've compiled a short list of candidates for you to consider.

Hannah had supplied me with a list of possible replacements? If it wasn't so shocking I would've laughed. I'd had the love of my life and I'd be foolish to believe it could happen twice in a lifetime.

Winter Adams

Remember Winter Adams, my cousin? She was a bridesmaid in our wedding. Winter has a big heart and she loves children. She'd make you a wonderful wife. She's also a chef and will cook you incredible meals. I want you to seriously consider her.

Of course I remembered Winter. We hadn't seen as much of Winter after she opened her restaurant, the French Café on Blossom Street. I liked Winter, but I had no intention of remarrying.

Leanne Lancaster

The second woman I want you to consider is Leanne Lancaster, my oncology nurse. I admire her emotional strength. She's divorced and had a rough time of it. My heart tells me she'd suit you. Meet with her, Michael, get to know her. That's all I ask.

Meet with Leanne...get to know her. I doubt Hannah had an inkling of what she was really asking. I had no interest whatever in seeking out this woman.

Macy Roth

The third person I want you to consider is Macy Roth. She's funny and clever. She models and paints murals and has two or three other jobs. I know she'll make you smile, Michael. I'm afraid that when I'm gone, you'll become far too serious. I want you to laugh and enjoy life.

Hannah was right; I hadn't laughed much in the past two years. But for her to suggest I remarry—and go so far as to name three women—was almost more than I could take in.

I've given you three names, Michael. Each is someone I know and trust. Any of them would make you a good wife and companion. Choose well.

Your loving wife,

Hannah

lace
SHAWL

Macy spent a lot of time thinking about her friend Hannah and knitting warm gifts for her. This pretty shawl was one of those gifts. She also sent drawings and wrote poems to cheer Hannah.

⬛⬛⬛◻ INTERMEDIATE

Finished Size: 22" x 61" (56 x 155 cm)

MATERIALS

Medium Weight Yarn
[1.75 ounces, 109 yards
(50 grams, 99 meters) per skein]:
  8 skeins
24" (61 cm) Circular knitting needle,
  size 9 (5.5 mm) **or** size needed for gauge

Techniques used: • YO *(Fig. 5, page 44)*;
• K2 tog *(Fig. 8, page 44)*; • SSK *(Figs. 9a-c, page 45)*; and • slip 1, K2 tog, PSSO *(Fig. 10, page 45)*.

GAUGE: In Stockinette Stitch,
     16 sts and 22 rows = 4" (10 cm)

SHAWL

Cast on 88 sts.

Row 1: (P1, K1) across.

Row 2 (Right side)**:** (K1, P1) across.

Rows 3-6: Repeat Rows 1 and 2 twice (Seed Stitch).

Row 7 AND ALL WRONG SIDE ROWS: (P1, K1) twice, purl across to last 3 sts, K1, P1, K1.

Row 8: (K1, P1) twice, K9, YO, SSK, K2, YO, SSK, knit across to last 19 sts, YO, SSK, K2, YO, SSK, K 10, P1, K1, P1.

Row 10: (K1, P1) twice, K7, K2 tog, YO, K1, YO, SSK, K2, YO, SSK, knit across to last 21 sts, K2 tog, YO, K1, YO, SSK, K2, YO, SSK, K9, P1, K1, P1.

Row 12: (K1, P1) twice, K6, K2 tog, YO, K3, YO, SSK, K2, YO, SSK, (K 10, YO, SSK) 3 times, K9, K2 tog, YO, K3, YO, SSK, K2, YO, SSK, K8, P1, K1, P1.

Row 14: (K1, P1) twice, K5, † K2 tog, YO, K2, K2 tog, YO, K1, YO, SSK, K2, YO, SSK, K7 †, (K2 tog, YO, K1, YO, SSK, K7) 3 times, repeat from † to † once, P1, K1, P1.

Row 16: (K1, P1) twice, K4, † K2 tog, YO, K2, K2 tog, YO, K3, YO, SSK, K2, YO, SSK †, K5, (K2 tog, YO, K3, YO, SSK, K5) 3 times, repeat from † to † once, K6, P1, K1, P1.

Row 18: (K1, P1) twice, † K6, YO, SSK, K2, YO, SSK, YO, K2 tog, YO, K2, K2 tog, YO, K2 tog †, [K6, YO, SSK, (YO, K2 tog) twice] 3 times, repeat from † to † once, K5, P1, K1, P1.

Row 20: (K1, P1) twice, K7, † YO, SSK, K2, YO, slip 1 as if to **knit**, K2 tog, PSSO, YO, K2, K2 tog, YO †, K9, (YO, slip 1 as if to **knit**, K2 tog, PSSO, YO, K9) 3 times, repeat from † to † once, K7, P1, K1, P1.

When Macy learned I was in the hospital, she brought me a big bouquet of daisies from her yard. She sent me notes of encouragement—cards she made herself with adorable sketches of her cats. And she knit me socks and a shawl I wore all the time.

—Hannah Everett

Hannah's List

Row 22: (K1, P1) twice, K8, † YO, SSK, K2, YO, SSK, K1, K2 tog, YO †, K 11, (YO, SSK, K 10) 3 times, repeat from † to † once, K8, P1, K1, P1.

Repeat Rows 7-22 for pattern until Shawl measures approximately 60" (152.5 cm) from cast on edge, ending by working Row 11.

Last 6 Rows: Repeat Row 2 once, then repeat Rows 1 and 2 twice; and then repeat Row 1 once **more**.

Bind off all sts in Seed Stitch.

Design by Cathy Hardy.

sammy's dog SWEATER

What do you do when a sweet-natured pup is looking to you for the comfort of a good home? If a stray turns up in Macy's neighborhood, it's sure to find its way into her house. As a knitter, Macy knows exactly what Sammy will need once the cool days of fall arrive.

⬤⬛⬛⬛◻ INTERMEDIATE

Size	Actual Chest Measurement	
Extra Small	12"	(30.5 cm)
Small	16"	(40.5 cm)
Medium	20"	(51 cm)
Large	24"	(61 cm)
Extra Large	28"	(71 cm)
2X-Large	32"	(81.5 cm)

Size Note: Choose the size closest to the actual chest measurement of your dog, measured behind the front legs. Instructions are written with sizes Extra Small, Small, and Medium in the first set of braces { } and sizes Large, Extra Large and 2X-Large in the second set of braces. Instructions will be easier to read if you circle all the numbers pertaining to your dog's size. If only one number is given, it applies to all sizes.

MATERIALS

Medium Weight Yarn ⓶④
[3.5 ounces, 190 yards (99 grams, 174 meters) per skein]:
   Teal - {1-1-1}{2-2-2} skein(s)
[7 ounces, 364 yards (198 grams, 333 meters) per skein]:
   Brown - 1 skein
Straight knitting needles, size 7 (4.5 mm) **or** size needed for gauge
Double pointed knitting needles, size 6 (4 mm) for I-Cord and 3-needle bind off
Yarn needle
Sewing needle and thread
¾" (19 mm) Button(s) - {1-1-1}{2-2-2}

Techniques used: • K2 tog *(Fig. 8, page 44)* and • YO *(Fig. 5, page 44)*.

GAUGE: In Stockinette Stitch and color pattern, 20 sts and 24 rows = 4" (10 cm)

Tip: To custom fit the sweater to your dog, measure the length of your dog's back from the tail to the base of the neck for the Body length of sweater. Measure from the base of the neck at your dog's side to the center front of neck for Front Chest Band length.

BODY

Note: Body width is slightly more than half of actual chest measurement.

Using Teal, cast on {35-47-55}{67-75-87} sts.

Row 1: Purl across.

Row 2 (Right side)**:** With Teal K3 *(Fig. 4, page 44)*, ★ with Brown K1, with Teal K3; repeat from ★ across.

Row 3: With Teal P4, with Brown P1, ★ with Teal P3, with Brown P1; repeat from ★ across to last 2 sts, with Teal P2.

Row 4: With Teal K2, with Brown K3, ★ with Teal K1, with Brown K3; repeat from ★ across to last 2 sts, with Teal K2.

Row 5: With Teal P2, with Brown P1, ★ with Teal P3, with Brown P1; repeat from ★ across to last 4 sts, with Teal P4.

Instructions continued on page 10.

A car horn blared not all that far away, followed by the sound of screeching tires. Peeking through the small front window, Macy saw the lights of a car illuminate a large dog who stood in the middle of the street. Macy hurried outside and grabbed the trembling dog by the scruff of his neck. His pitiful brown eyes seemed to thank her for coming to his rescue.

—*Hannah's List*

Repeat Rows 2-5 for pattern until Body measures approximately {6¼-8¾-11½}{13½-15½-17½}"/{16-22-29}{34.5-39.5-44.5} cm from cast on edge **or** to desired length to base of neck, ending by working a **purl** row.

FRONT CHEST BAND

Both sides of the Neck are worked at the same time using separate yarns for **each** side.

Note: It takes two stitches to bind off the first stitch.

Row 1: Working in established color pattern, knit across {11-15-15}{19-23-27} sts; with Teal, bind off center {13-17-25}{29-29-33} sts; knit across: {11-15-15}{19-23-27} sts **each** side.

Work even until Bands are two thirds the desired length, ending by working a **purl** row; cut Brown on each side.

Using Teal, continue working in Stockinette Stitch until Bands are desired length, ending by working a **purl** row. They should be long enough to slip comfortably over your dog's head when they are joined, and also fit around your dog's neck.

Slip the stitches from the first side onto an empty needle. Using a double pointed needle to join the Band stitches, work 3-Needle Bind-off *(Fig. 16, page 46)*.

BELLY BAND

Using Teal, cast on {7-9-11}{15-17-19} sts.

Knit 4 rows.

SIZES EXTRA SMALL, SMALL AND MEDIUM ONLY

Buttonhole Row: K{2-3-4}, K2 tog, YO, knit across.

SIZES LARGE, EXTRA LARGE AND 2X-LARGE ONLY

Buttonhole Row: K2, K2 tog, YO, K{6-8-10}, K2 tog, YO, K3.

ALL SIZES

Knit every row until Belly Band measures approximately {5-6½-8½}{10½-12½-14½}"/{12.5-16.5-21.5}{26.5-32-37} cm from cast on edge **or** to desired length.

Bind off all sts leaving a long end for sewing.

FINISHING
ATTACHED I-CORD EDGING

Work attached I-Cord Edging around outer edge of sweater, then around neck edge as follows:

Using double pointed needles and Teal, cast on 3 sts.

★ K2, slip 1 as if to **purl**, with **wrong** side of Sweater facing, pick up one st on edge *(Figs. 13a & b, page 45)*, pass slipped st over picked up st, slide sts to opposite end of needle; repeat from ★ around entire edge skipping rows or sts as necessary to keep the edging from being too full.

Bind off all sts in **knit**; cut yarn leaving a long end for sewing.

Sew ends of Edging together.

Place the Sweater on your dog and mark placement for Belly Band. Sew bound off edge of Belly Band to side of Body, placing it under the Edging.

Sew button(s) to Sweater to correspond with buttonhole(s).

Block sweater *(see Blocking, page 46)*.

Design by Sarah J. Green.

BUTTERFLY

This quick-to-knit butterfly is one of Macy's favorite patterns to make for her feline friends. There are probably a half-dozen of the brightly colored soft toys hidden behind sofa cushions and under the furniture at Macy's house.

● ■ □ □ **EASY**

Finished Size: approximately 4¹/₂" wide (11.5 cm)

MATERIALS
　100% Cotton Medium Weight Yarn
　　Main Color (Yellow or Variegated) -
　　　15 yards (13.5 meters) **each**
　　Black - 4 yards (3.5 meters) **each**
　Straight knitting needles, size 8 (5 mm)
　18 mm Craft bell - 1 **each**
　Yarn needle

Gauge is not of great importance.

TOP WING (Make 2)
Using Main Color, cast on 12 sts.

Rows 1-10: Knit across.

Cut yarn leaving a long end for sewing and thread yarn needle with end. Slip stitches onto yarn needle and draw through, then draw through the stitches a second time; draw up **tightly**; leave end for sewing Wing to Body.

BOTTOM WING (Make 2)
Using Main Color, cast on 6 sts.

Rows 1-6: Knit across.

Cut yarn leaving a long end for sewing and thread yarn needle with end. Slip stitches onto yarn needle and draw through, then draw through the stitches a second time; draw up **tightly**; leave end for sewing Wing to Body.

BODY
Using Black, cast on 6 sts.

Row 1: Purl across.

Row 2: Knit across.

Rows 3-10: Repeat Rows 1 and 2, 4 times.

Cut yarn leaving a long end for sewing and thread yarn needle with end. Slip stitches onto yarn needle and draw through; then sew ends of rows together, do **not** cut end.

Stuff Body with Black yarn. Sew cast on edge together, then using same yarn end, sew bell to seam, wrapping yarn around shank of bell several times before securing end.

Using photo as a guide, sew Wings to Body.

Design by Sarah J. Green.

sculptured PILLOWS

Michael can't remember who knitted the pair of pillows for Hannah. In fact, he wasn't really thinking about going through Hannah's things at all—at least, not until he sat down to visit Winter, Hannah's cousin. When he thought of what Hannah's letter asked of him, he couldn't think of anything else to say.

Finished Size: 12" (30.5 cm) square

MATERIALS

Medium Weight Yarn
[3.5 ounces, 220 yards
(100 grams, 201 meters) per hank]:
  2 hanks for **each** Pillow
16" (40.5 cm) **and** 24" (61 cm) Circular
  knitting needles, size 8 (5 mm) **or** size
  needed for gauge
Cable needle (for Traveling Cables)
Markers
Yarn needle
Pillow form(s) - 12" (30.5 cm) square **each**

Techniques used: • K2 tog *(Fig. 8, page 44)*
and • SSK *(Figs. 9a-c, page 45)*.

GAUGE: In Stockinette Stitch,
        18 sts and 24 rnds = 4" (10 cm)

Each Square is knit in the round *(see Using Circular Needle, page 43).*

Tip: As the stitch count decreases and the rounds become smaller, change to 16" (40.5 cm) circular knitting needle.

Tip: To achieve even corner miters, it is important to keep good tension. After working a decrease, insert the needle into the next stitch and tighten by pulling firmly on the working yarn, then complete the stitch.

8 POINT FLOWER

◖◼◻◻ EASY

SQUARE (Make 2)
Using 24" (61 cm) circular knitting needle, ★ cast on 54 sts, place marker *(see Markers, page 43)*; repeat from ★ 3 times **more**: 216 sts.

Note: The last marker placed indicates the beginning of the round.

Rnd 1 (Right side - Decrease rnd): ★ K2 tog, knit across to within 2 sts of next marker, SSK; repeat from ★ around: 208 sts.

Rnd 2: Purl around.

Rnd 3: Repeat Rnd 1: 200 sts.

Rnd 4: Purl around.

Rnds 5-7: Repeat Rnd 1, 3 times: 176 sts.

Rnd 8: Knit around.

Rnd 9: Repeat Rnd 1: 168 sts.

Rnds 10 and 11: Purl around.

Rnds 12-14: Repeat Rnd 1, 3 times: 144 sts.

Rnd 15: Knit around.

Rnd 16: Repeat Rnd 1: 136 sts.

Rnds 17-19: Purl around.

Instructions continued on page 14.

I entered the French Café, where I saw Winter right away. Although I looked hard for a resemblance to Hannah, I didn't see any.

"Come sit over here." Winter led me to a table by the window.

"You have a nice place," I commented. I stared down into my coffee. "It's hard to believe Hannah's been gone a year."

"It is," Winter agreed quietly.

"I'm starting to clear out her things. I wondered if there was anything of hers you'd like to have?"

Winter's eyes misted. "Oh, Michael, that's so thoughtful of you."

—Michael Everett
Hannah's List

Rnds 20-22: Repeat Rnd 1, 3 times: 112 sts.

Rnd 23: Knit around.

Rnd 24: Repeat Rnd 1: 104 sts.

Rnd 25: Purl around.

Rnds 26-28: Repeat Rnd 1, 3 times: 80 sts.

Rnd 29: Knit around.

Rnd 30: Repeat Rnd 1: 72 sts.

Rnds 31-33: Purl around.

Rnds 34 and 35: Repeat Rnd 1 twice: 56 sts.

Rnd 36: Keeping first marker in place to indicate beginning of rnd, knit around removing remaining markers.

Rnds 37-45: Knit around.

Rnd 46: Purl around.

Rnd 47: Knit around.

Rnd 48: Purl around.

Cut yarn leaving a long end, then push yarn end through center opening to the **wrong** side.

CENTER WEAVING
This procedure allows the design to become dimensional. Slide all of the stitches onto the cable portion of the circular needle. This allows room for the yarn needle to pass through the stitches more easily.

RIGHT SIDE
Thread the yarn needle with an 18" (45.5 cm) length of yarn.
With **right** side of Square facing and working from **right** to **left** (as if to purl), insert the yarn needle through the stitches as follows:

8 Point Flower - Insert needle through first 2 sts, skip next 3 sts, (insert needle through next 4 sts, skip next 3 sts) 7 times, insert needle through last 2 sts.

Pull the yarn through, leaving a 3" (7.5 cm) end at the beginning; remove the yarn needle.

WRONG SIDE
Rethread the yarn needle with an 18" (45.5 cm) length of yarn.
With **right** side of piece facing, roll the stitches forward to expose the **wrong** side of the stitches; working from **right** to **left**, weave the yarn through the stitches as follows:

8 Point Flower - Skip first 2 sts, insert needle through next 3 sts, (skip next 4 sts, insert needle through next 3 sts) 7 times, skip last 2 sts.

Pull the yarn through, leaving a 3" (7.5 cm) end at the beginning; remove the yarn needle.

Make sure the yarn has been woven through **each** stitch, then remove the circular needle.

Push the wrong side yarn ends through the center opening and turn the square over. Gather all wrong side stitches up tightly by pulling on the yarn ends; tie a knot. Turn the square over and gather all right side stitches tightly by pulling on the yarn ends; tie a knot. Thread the yarn needle with the right side yarn ends and pass through the center to the wrong side. Turn the square over and tie all of the yarn ends together. Weave in all the ends on wrong side.

This gathering process creates ridges with the right side stitches and valleys with the wrong side stitches. Using the photo as a guide, sculpt your squares by gently shaping the ridges and the valleys.

ASSEMBLY

With **wrong** sides together and working through **both** loops of cast on edge on **both** Squares, sew pieces together forming a ridge and inserting pillow form before closing.

TRAVELING CABLES

◖■■■▭ INTERMEDIATE

STITCH GUIDE

FRONT CABLE (uses 4 sts)
Slip next 2 sts onto cable needle and hold in **front** of work, K2 from left needle, K2 from cable needle.

BACK CABLE (uses 4 sts)
Slip next 2 sts onto cable needle and hold in **back** of work, K2 from left needle, K2 from cable needle.

SQUARE (Make 2)

Work same as 8 Point Flower, page 12, through Rnd 33: 72 sts.

Rnd 34: Repeat Rnd 1: 64 sts.

Rnd 35: (Work Front Cable, K8, work Back Cable) around.

Rnds 36 and 37: Knit around.

Rnd 38: K2, work Front Cable, K4, work Back Cable, ★ K4, work Front Cable, K4, work Back Cable; repeat from ★ 2 times **more**, K2.

Rnds 39 and 40: Knit around.

Rnd 41: K4, work Front Cable, work Back Cable, (K8, work Front Cable, work Back Cable) 3 times, K4.

Rnds 42 and 43: Knit around.

Rnds 44 and 45: Repeat Rnd 1 twice: 48 sts.

Rnd 46: Keeping first marker in place to indicate beginning of rnd, knit around removing remaining markers.

Rnds 47 and 48: Knit around.

Cut yarn leaving a long end, then push yarn end through center opening to the **wrong** side.

CENTER WEAVING

Work same as 8 Point Flower, page 14, working through stitches as follows:

Right side of Traveling Cable - Skip first 3 sts, insert needle through next 6 sts, (skip next 6 sts, insert needle through next 6 sts) 3 times, skip last 3 sts.

Wrong side of Traveling Cable - Insert needle through first 3 sts, skip next 6 sts, (insert needle through next 6 sts, skip next 6 sts) 3 times, insert needle through last 3 sts.

ASSEMBLY

With **wrong** sides together and working through **both** loops of cast on edge on **both** Squares, sew pieces together forming a ridge and inserting pillow form before closing.

Designs by Leslie Calaway.

AFGHAN

Leanne stays busy with her work as a nurse, and it lifts her spirits when friends do nice things like giving her a hand-knit afghan. Lately Leanne is beginning to look ahead to the future—perhaps toward rebuilding her life with a man like Michael Everett.

◀■□□ EASY

Finished Size: 47¹/₂" x 63¹/₂" (120.5 cm x 161.5 cm)

MATERIALS
Medium Weight Yarn
[3.5 ounces, 208 yards
(100 grams, 190 meters) per skein]:
   16 skeins
36" (91.5 cm) Circular knitting needles, sizes
   10¹/₂ (6.5 mm) **and** 11 (8 mm) **or** sizes
   needed for gauge

> Afghan is worked holding 2 strands of yarn together throughout.

GAUGE: With larger size needle, in pattern,
   28 sts (2 repeats) = 9" (22.75 cm);
   24 rows (2 repeats) = 5¹/₂" (14 cm)

Gauge Swatch: 11¹/₂"w x 5¹/₂"h
   (29.25 cm x 14 cm)
Using larger size needle, cast on 36 sts.
Work same as Body for 24 rows.
Bind off all sts.

BOTTOM BORDER
Using smaller size needle, cast on 148 sts.

Rows 1-6: Knit across.

BODY
Change to larger size needle.

Row 1: K7, P8, (K6, P8) across to last 7 sts, K7.

Row 2 (Right side): Knit across.

Rows 3-5: Repeat Rows 1 and 2 once, then repeat Row 1 once **more**.

Row 6: (K6, P2) twice, (K4, P2, K6, P2) across to last 6 sts, K6.

Row 7: K4, P3, K2, P4, K2, (P6, K2, P4, K2) across to last 7 sts, P3, K4.

Row 8: K8, (P2, K2, P2, K8) across.

Row 9: K4, P5, K4, (P 10, K4) across to last 9 sts, P5, K4.

Row 10: K8, (P2, K2, P2, K8) across.

Row 11: K4, P3, K2, P4, K2, (P6, K2, P4, K2) across to last 7 sts, P3, K4.

Row 12: (K6, P2) twice, (K4, P2, K6, P2) across to last 6 sts, K6.

Repeat Rows 1-12 for pattern until Afghan measures approximately 62¹/₂" (159 cm) from cast on edge, ending by working Row 5.

TOP BORDER
Change to smaller size needle.

Rows 1-5: Knit across.

With larger size needle, bind off all sts in **knit**.

Design by Linda Daley.

"Do you think it'd be okay if I called you sometime?" I could hardly believe I was asking. And yet it felt right. I wasn't ready to date and she didn't appear to be, either. Maybe if we met casually a few times it would help both of us ease back into the world of the living. Leanne looked up at me and grinned. "I think that would be a good idea."

—Michael Everett
Hannah's List

harvey's VEST

Harvey isn't going to like the sweater vest that Macy's knitting for him—at least, that's what he'll be sure to tell her! But Macy knows that being cantankerous is how her elderly neighbor deals with emotions. Truth is, Harvey will enjoy the vest the same way he does Macy's casseroles—very much—as long as she isn't looking.

◀■■■▢ INTERMEDIATE

Size	Finished Chest Measurement	
34	36½"	(92.5 cm)
36	38"	(96.5 cm)
38	40"	(101.5 cm)
40	42½"	(108 cm)
42	44"	(112 cm)
44	46"	(117 cm)

Size Note: Instructions are written with sizes 34, 36, and 38 in the first set of braces { } and sizes 40, 42, and 44 in the second set of braces. Instructions will be easier to read if you circle all the numbers pertaining to your size. If only one number is given, it applies to all sizes.

MATERIALS

Medium Weight Yarn
[3.5 ounces, 223 yards
(100 grams, 205 meters) per skein]:
   {4-4-4}{5-5-5} skeins
Straight knitting needles, size 8 (5 mm) **or** size needed for gauge
29" (73.5 cm) Circular knitting needle, size 8 (5 mm)
Markers
Yarn needle
¾"(19 mm) Buttons - 5
Sewing needle and thread

Techniques used: • P2 tog *(Fig. 11, page 45)*; • SSP *(Fig. 12, page 45)*; • SSK *(Figs. 9a-c, page 45)*; • K2 tog *(Fig. 8, page 44)*; and • YO *(Fig. 5, page 44)*.

GAUGE: In pattern,
   19 sts and 28 rows = 4" (10 cm)

Gauge Swatch: 4" (10 cm) square
Cast on 19 sts.
Work same as Back for 28 rows.
Bind off all sts.

BACK

Cast on {89-93-97}{103-107-111} sts.

Rows 1-8: Knit across.

Row 9: P2, K1, (P1, K1) across to last 2 sts, P2.

Row 10 (Right side): K2, P1, (K1, P1) across to last 2 sts, K2.

Rows 11 and 12: Knit across.

Repeat Rows 9-12 for pattern until piece measures approximately {14-14½-14½}{15-15-15½}"/{35.5-37-37}{38-38-39.5} cm from cast on edge, ending by working Row 10.

ARMHOLE SHAPING

Maintain established pattern throughout.

Rows 1 and 2: Bind off {7-7-8}{10-10-11} sts, knit across: {75-79-81}{83-87-89} sts.

Row 3: P1, P2 tog, work across to last 3 sts, SSP, P1: {73-77-79}{81-85-87} sts.

Row 4: K1, SSK, work across to last 3 sts, K2 tog, K1: {71-75-77}{79-83-85} sts.

Macy tried to conform whenever possible, but she wasn't very successful. Her problem was the fact that she got bored if she had to do only one thing for any length of time. It was the same with knitting. She had probably a dozen half-completed projects lying around. The vest for Harvey was the current one, and she was determined to get that done by the fall.

—Hannah's List

Row 5: K1, K2 tog, knit across to last 3 sts, SSK, K1: {69-73-75}{77-81-83} sts.

Row 6: K1, SSK, knit across to last 3 sts, K2 tog, K1: {67-71-73}{75-79-81} sts.

Row 7: P1, P2 tog, work across to last 3 sts, SSP, P1: {65-69-71}{73-77-79} sts.

Work even until Armholes measure approximately {9$\frac{1}{2}$-9$\frac{3}{4}$-10}{10$\frac{3}{4}$-10$\frac{3}{4}$-11}"/ {24-25-25.5}{27.5-27.5-28} cm, ending by working a **right** side row.

Instructions continued on page 20.

SHOULDER SHAPING

Rows 1-4: Bind off {6-6-6}{6-6-7} sts, work across: {41-45-47}{49-53-51} sts.

Rows 5 and 6: Bind off {5-6-5}{5-7-6} sts, work across: {31-33-37}{39-39-39} sts.

Bind off remaining sts in pattern.

RIGHT FRONT

Cast on {41-43-45}{49-51-53} sts.

Work same as Back to Armhole Shaping.

ARMHOLE & NECK SHAPING

Maintain established pattern throughout.

Row 1: Bind off {7-7-8}{10-10-11} sts, knit across: {34-36-37}{39-41-42} sts.

Row 2: Knit across to last 3 sts, K2 tog, K1: {33-35-36}{38-40-41} sts.

Row 3: P1, P2 tog, work across: {32-34-35}{37-39-40} sts.

Row 4: K1, SSK, work across to last 3 sts, K2 tog, K1: {30-32-33}{35-37-38} sts.

Row 5: K1, K2 tog, knit across: {29-31-32}{34-36-37} sts.

Row 6: Knit across to last 3 sts, K2 tog, K1: {28-30-31}{33-35-36} sts.

Row 7: Work across.

Row 8 (Neck decrease row)**:** K1, SSK, work across: {27-29-30}{32-34-35} sts.

Continue to decrease one stitch at Neck edge, every fourth row, {5-7-12}{15-15-15} times **more**; then decrease every sixth row, {5-4-1}{0-0-0} time(s) **(see Zeros, page 43):** {17-18-17}{17-19-20} sts.

Work even until Right Front measures same as Back to Shoulder Shaping, ending by working a **right** side row.

SHOULDER SHAPING

Row 1: Bind off {6-6-6}{6-6-7} sts, work across: {11-12-11}{11-13-13} sts.

Row 2: Work across.

Rows 3 and 4: Repeat Rows 1 and 2: {5-6-5}{5-7-6} sts.

Bind off remaining sts in pattern leaving a long end for sewing.

LEFT FRONT

Cast on {41-43-45}{49-51-53} sts.

Work same as Back to Armhole Shaping, ending by working Row 9.

ARMHOLE & NECK SHAPING

Maintain established pattern throughout.

Row 1: Bind off {7-7-8}{10-10-11} sts, work across: {34-36-37}{39-41-42} sts.

Row 2: Knit across.

Row 3: K1, SSK, knit across to last 3 sts, K2 tog, K1: {32-34-35}{37-39-40} sts.

Row 4: Work across to last 3 sts, SSP, P1: {31-33-34}{36-38-39} sts.

Row 5: K1, SSK, work across: {30-32-33} {35-37-38} sts.

Row 6: Knit across to last 3 sts, SSK, K1: {29-31-32}{34-36-37} sts.

Row 7: K1, SSK, knit across to last 3 sts, K2 tog, K1: {27-29-30}{32-34-35} sts.

Continue to decrease one stitch at Neck edge, every fourth row, {5-7-12}{15-15-15} times **more**; then decrease every sixth row, {5-4-1}{0-0-0} time(s): {17-18-17}{17-19-20} sts.

Work even until Left Front measures same as Back to Shoulder Shaping, ending by working a **wrong** side row.

SHOULDER SHAPING
Work same as Right Front.

FINISHING
Using long ends, sew shoulder seams.

FRONT BAND
With **right** side facing and using circular needle, pick up {64-66-66}{68-68-70} sts evenly spaced along Right Front edge to Neck Shaping **(Figs. 13a & b, page 45)**, pick up {46-48-50}{54-54-56} sts evenly spaced along Neck Shaping, pick up {31-33-37}{39-39-39} sts across Back Neck edge, pick up {46-48-50}{54-54-56} sts evenly spaced along Left Front Neck Shaping, pick up {64-66-66}{68-68-70} sts evenly spaced along Left Front edge: {251-261-269}{283-283-291} sts.

Rows 1-3: Knit across.

Place markers on Left Front for buttonholes, placing first marker approximately ³/4" (19 mm) above cast on edge and last marker at beginning of Neck Shaping, then evenly spacing markers for remaining 3 buttonholes.

Row 4 (Buttonhole row)**:** Knit across to first marker, K2 tog, YO, ★ knit across to next marker, K2 tog, YO; repeat from ★ 3 times **more**, knit across.

Rows 5-8: Knit across.

Bind off all sts in **knit**.

ARMHOLE BAND
With **right** side facing and using circular needle, pick up {96-98-102}{114-114-118} sts evenly spaced along Armhole edge.

Rows 1-8: Knit across.

Bind off all sts in **knit**.

Repeat on remaining Armhole.

Weave side seams **(Fig. 14, page 46)**.

Sew buttons to Right Front opposite buttonholes.

Design by Sarah J. Green.

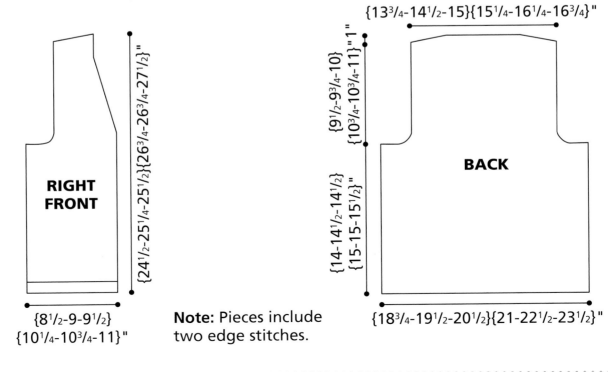

RIGHT FRONT

{24¹/2-25¹/4-25¹/2}{26³/4-26³/4-27¹/2}"

{8¹/2-9-9¹/2}
{10¹/4-10³/4-11}"

Note: Pieces include two edge stitches.

BACK

{13³/4-14¹/2-15}{15¹/4-16¹/4-16³/4}"

{9¹/2-9³/4-10}{10³/4-10³/4-11}"1"

{14-14¹/2-14¹/2}{15-15-15¹/2}"

{18³/4-19¹/2-20¹/2}{21-22¹/2-23¹/2}"

harvey's crew SOCKS

For Macy, knitting a pair of socks is at least a two-part job. When the first sock is finished, it's likely to get misplaced. However, because she does spend a good deal of time worrying about Harvey, Macy got both socks completed in record time.

⬤⬤⬤◻ INTERMEDIATE

Size	Finished Foot Circumference	
Small	8¹/₂"	(21.5 cm)
Medium	9¹/₂"	(24 cm)
Large	10¹/₄"	(26 cm)

Size Note: Instructions are written for size Small with sizes Medium and Large in braces { }. Instructions will be easier to read if you circle all the numbers pertaining to your size. If only one number is given, it applies to all sizes.

MATERIALS
Super Fine Weight Yarn **SUPER FINE 1**
[1.75 ounces, 166 yards (50 grams, 152 meters) per skein]: 3{3-4} skeins
Set of 5 double pointed knitting needles, sizes 3 (3.25 mm) **and** 4 (3.5 mm) **or** sizes needed for gauge
Stitch holders - 2
Split-ring marker
Tapestry needle

Techniques used: • P2 tog *(Fig. 11, page 45)*; • SSK *(Figs. 9a-c, page 45)*; and • K2 tog *(Fig. 8, page 44)*.

GAUGE: With **smaller** size needles, in Stockinette Stitch, 28 sts and 36 rnds = 4" (10 cm)

RIBBING
Using larger size needles, cast on 60{66-72} sts.

Divide the sts onto 4 needles *(see Double Pointed Needles, page 43)*, placing 15{16-18} sts on the first needle, 15{17-18} sts on the second and third needles, and 15{16-18} sts on the fourth needle.

Tip: The yarn end indicates the beginning of the round.

Rnds 1-9: (P2, K4) around.

LEG
Change to smaller size needles.

Rnd 1: Knit around.

Rnd 2: K3, P2, (K4, P2) around to last st, K1.

Rnds 3-10: Repeat Rnds 1 and 2, 4 times.

Rnd 11: Knit around.

Rnd 12: (P2, K4) around.

Rnds 13-20: Repeat Rnds 11 and 12, 4 times.

Repeat Rnds 1-20 until sock measures approximately 6¹/₂{7-7¹/₂}"/16.5{18-19} cm from cast on edge **or** 1" (2.5 cm) less than desired length.

Knit each round (Stockinette Stitch) for 1" (2.5 cm).

Macy took a shortcut across the lawn to Harvey's place. The World War II veteran had been her grandmother's next-door neighbor for more than forty years. They'd been good friends all that time. Macy was convinced they were "sweet" on each other.

—*Hannah's List*

HEEL FLAP

Dividing Stitches: Knit across first needle; slip sts from the next 2 needles onto 2 separate st holders for Instep to be worked later.

Tip: The following pattern will make the Heel dense and will help prevent it from wearing out.

When instructed to slip a stitch, always slip as if to **purl** with yarn held to **wrong** side so that the carried strand won't show on the right side.

With **wrong** side facing, work Row 1 across both needles onto one needle. The Heel Flap will be worked back and forth across these 30{32-36} sts.

Row 1: ★ Slip 1, P1; repeat from ★ across.

Row 2: ★ Slip 1, K1; repeat from ★ across.

Rows 3 thru 30{32-36}: Repeat Rows 1 and 2, 14{15-17} times.

Instructions continued on page 27.

hannah's ankle
SOCKS

When Michael expresses disbelief that she was a good friend to his late wife, Macy is surprised. However, she's simply not the kind of person who lingers over a hurt. In fact, if anyone is going to take an insult and turn it into something good, it's Macy Roth.

⬤⬤⬤◐◯ INTERMEDIATE

Size	Finished Foot Circumference	
Small	7"	(18 cm)
Medium	8"	(20.5 cm)
Large	9"	(23 cm)

Size Note: Instructions are written for size Small with sizes Medium and Large in braces { }. Instructions will be easier to read if you circle all the numbers pertaining to your size. If only one number is given, it applies to all sizes.

MATERIALS

Super Fine Weight Yarn
[1.76 ounces, 213 yards
(50 grams, 195 meters) per skein]:
   Main Color - 2 skeins
   Contrasting Color (Cuff) - 1 skein
Set of 5 double pointed knitting needles,
   size 1 (2.25 mm) **or** size needed for gauge
Stitch holders - 2
Split-ring marker
Tapestry needle

Techniques used: • P2 tog *(Fig. 11, page 45)*; • SSK *(Figs. 9a-c, page 45)*; and • K2 tog *(Fig. 8, page 44)*.

GAUGE: In Stockinette Stitch,
      36 sts and 48 rnds = 4" (10 cm)

CUFF

Using Contrasting Color, cast on 64{72-80} sts.

Divide sts onto 4 needles *(see Double Pointed Needles, page 43)*, placing 16{18-20} sts on each needle.

Tip: The Cuff is worked with the wrong side facing, since it will be turned down. The yarn end indicates the beginning of the round.

Rnds 1 and 2: (K2, P2) around.

Rnds 3 and 4: Purl around.

Rnds 5 and 6: (P2, K2) around.

Rnds 7 and 8: Purl around.

Repeat Rnds 1-8 until Cuff measures approximately 4" (10 cm) from cast on edge.

Cut Contrasting Color.

LEG

Using Main Color, knit each round until sock measures approximately 7" (18 cm) from cast on edge **or** to desired length.

HEEL FLAP

Dividing Stitches: Knit across first needle; slip sts from the next 2 needles onto 2 separate st holders for Instep to be worked later.

Tip: The following pattern will make the Heel dense and will help prevent it from wearing out.

"I wrote Hannah poems and mailed her letters and pictures of Snowball and Lovie," said Macy. "And I knit her socks. And a shawl."

I frowned. I remembered those multicolored socks and the letters; they'd made Hannah smile, when it didn't seem possible I'd ever see her smile again. Without my knowing it, Macy had given me a gift I'd never expected.

—Michael Everett
Hannah's List

When instructed to slip a stitch, always slip as if to **purl** with yarn held **loosely** to **right** side so that the carried strand shows on the right side forming the woven look.

With **wrong** side facing, work Row 1 across both needles onto one needle. The Heel Flap will be worked back and forth across these 32{36-40} sts.

Row 1: ★ Slip 1, P1; repeat from ★ across.

Row 2: ★ Slip 1, K1; repeat from ★ across.

Rows 3 thru 32{36-40}: Repeat Rows 1 and 2, 15{17-19} times.

Instructions continued on page 26.

TURN HEEL
Begin working in short rows as follows:

Row 1: P 19{21-23}, P2 tog, P1, leave remaining 10{12-14} sts unworked; **turn**.

Row 2: Slip 1, K7, SSK, K1, leave remaining 10{12-14} sts unworked; turn.

Row 3: Slip 1, P8, P2 tog, P1; turn.

Row 4: Slip 1, K9, SSK, K1; turn.

Rows 5 thru 12{14-16}: Repeat Rows 3 and 4, 4{5-6} times adding one st before decrease on each row: 20{22-24} sts.

GUSSET
The remainder of the sock will be worked in rounds.

Slip the Instep sts from the st holders onto 2 double pointed needles, 16{18-20} sts each.

FOUNDATION ROUND
With **right** side of Heel facing, using the same double pointed needle and continuing with the working yarn, pick up 16{18-20} sts along the side of the Heel Flap *(Fig. 13a, page 45)* and one st in the corner.
With separate needles, knit across the Instep sts (needles 2 and 3).
With an empty needle, pick up one st in the corner and 16{18-20} sts along the side of the Heel Flap. With the same needle, knit 10{11-12} Heel sts (this will be needle 4). Place a split-ring marker around the next st to indicate the beginning of the round *(see Markers, page 43)*.

Stitch count is 27{30-33} sts on the first needle, 16{18-20} sts on each of the second and third needles, and 27{30-33} sts on the fourth needle for a total of 86{96-106} sts.

GUSSET DECREASES
Rnd 1 (Decrease rnd)**:** Knit across the first needle to last 3 sts, K2 tog, K1; knit across the second and third needles; on the fourth needle, K1, SSK, knit across: 84{94-104} sts.

Rnd 2: Knit around.

Rnds 3 thru 22{24-26}: Repeat Rnds 1 and 2, 10{11-12} times: total of 64{72-80} sts, 16{18-20} sts on each needle.

FOOT
Work even, knitting each round, until Foot measures approximately 6$\frac{1}{2}${7$\frac{1}{2}$-8}"/ 16.5{19-20.5} cm from back of Heel **or** 1$\frac{3}{4}${2-2}"/4.5{5-5} cm less than total desired Foot length from back of Heel to Toe.

TOE
Rnd 1 (Decrease rnd)**:** Knit across first needle to last 3 sts, K2 tog, K1; on second needle, K1, SSK, knit across; on third needle, knit across to last 3 sts, K2 tog, K1; on fourth needle, K1, SSK, knit across: 15{17-19} sts on each needle.

Rnd 2: Knit around.

Rnds 3 thru 20{24-24}: Repeat Rnds 1 and 2, 9{11-11} times: 6{6-8} sts on each needle.

Using the fourth needle, knit across the sts on the first needle; cut yarn leaving a long end for grafting.

Slip the stitches from the third needle onto the second needle, so there are 12{12-16} sts on each of two needles.

Graft the remaining sts together *(Figs. 15a & b, page 46)*.

Repeat for second Sock.

Design by Cathy Hardy.

harvey's crew
SOCKS

continued from page 23.

TURN HEEL
Begin working in short rows as follows:

Row 1: P 17{19-21}, P2 tog, P1, leave remaining 10{10-12} sts unworked; **turn.**

Row 2: Slip 1, K5{7-7}, SSK, K1, leave remaining 10{10-12} sts unworked; turn.

Row 3: Slip 1, P6{8-8}, P2 tog, P1; turn.

Row 4: Slip 1, K7{9-9}, SSK, K1; turn.

Rows 5 thru 12{12-14}: Repeat Rows 3 and 4, 4{4-5} times adding one st before decrease on each row: 18{20-22} sts.

GUSSET
The remainder of the sock will be worked in rounds.

Slip the Instep sts from the st holders onto 2 double pointed needles, 15{17-18} sts each.

FOUNDATION ROUND
With **right** side of Heel facing, using the same double pointed needle and continuing with the working yarn, pick up 15{16-18} sts along the side of the Heel Flap *(Fig. 13a, page 45)* and one st in the corner.
With separate needles, knit across the Instep sts (needles 2 and 3).
With an empty needle, pick up one st in the corner and 15{16-18} sts along the side of the Heel Flap. With the same needle, knit 9{10-11} Heel sts (this will be needle 4). Place a split-ring marker around the next st to indicate the beginning of the round *(see Markers, page 43)*.

Stitch count is 25{27-30} sts on the first needle, 15{17-18} sts on each of the second and third needles, and 25{27-30} sts on the fourth needle for a total of 80{88-96} sts.

GUSSET DECREASES
Rnd 1 (Decrease rnd)**:** Knit across the first needle to last 3 sts, K2 tog, K1; knit across the second and third needles; on fourth needle, K1, SSK, knit across: 78{86-94} sts.

Rnd 2: Knit around.

Rnds 3 thru 20{22-24}: Repeat Rnds 1 and 2, 9{10-11} times: 60{66-72} sts.

FOOT
Work even, knitting each round, until Foot measures approximately 8$\frac{1}{2}${8$\frac{3}{4}$-9}"/21.5{22-23} cm from back of Heel **or** 2{2$\frac{1}{4}$-2$\frac{1}{2}$}"/5{5.5-6.5} cm less than total desired Foot length from back of Heel to Toe.

TOE
For Medium size only, slip one stitch from the second needle onto the first needle.

Rnd 1 (Decrease rnd)**:** Knit across first needle to last 3 sts, K2 tog, K1; on second needle, K1, SSK, knit across; on third needle, knit across to last 3 sts, K2 tog, K1; on fourth needle, K1, SSK, knit across: 56{62-68} sts.

Rnd 2: Knit around.

Rnds 3 thru 18{20-22}: Repeat Rnds 1 and 2, 8{9-10} times: 24{26-28} sts.

Using the fourth needle, knit across the sts on the first needle; cut yarn leaving a long end for grafting.

Slip the stitches from the third needle onto the second needle, so there are 12{13-14} sts on each of two needles.

Graft the remaining sts together *(Figs. 15a & b, page 46)*.

Repeat for second Sock.

Design by Cathy Hardy.

stylish
SCARF

Whether she's painting or knitting, Macy is always fond of color. When she was asked to model this scarf for a popular yarn company, she liked the pretty shade of orange. It may be the next knitting project she tackles. After all, if you've already got a dozen projects going, what's one more?

◀■■■▷ INTERMEDIATE

Finished Size: 7¹/₂" x 50" (19 cm x 127 cm)

MATERIALS
Medium Weight Yarn MEDIUM 4
[3.5 ounces, 219 yards
(100 grams, 200 meters) per hank]:
  2 hanks
Straight knitting needles, size 7 (4.5 mm)
  or size needed for gauge

Techniques used: • YO *(Fig. 5, page 44)*; • K2 tog *(Fig. 8, page 44)*; • SSK *(Figs. 9a-c, page 45)*; and • slip 1, K2 tog, PSSO *(Fig. 10, page 45)*.

GAUGE: In Garter Stitch (purl every row),
        9 sts = 2" (5 cm)

SCARF
Cast on 43 sts.

Row 1: Purl across.

Row 2 (Right side)**:** K1, † SSK, K1, P6, K2, YO, K1, YO, K2, P2, K1, K2 tog †, P3, repeat from † to † once, K1.

Row 3 AND ALL WRONG SIDE ROWS: Purl across.

Row 4: K1, † SSK, K1, P5, K2, YO, K1, YO, K2, P3, K1, K2 tog †, K3, repeat from † to † once, K1.

Row 6: K1, † SSK, K1, P4, K2, YO, K1, YO, K2, P4, K1, K2 tog †, YO, slip 1 as if to **knit**, K2 tog, PSSO, YO, repeat from † to † once, K1.

Row 8: K1, † SSK, K1, P3, K2, YO, K1, YO, K2, P5, K1, K2 tog †, K3, repeat from † to † once, K1.

Row 10: K1, † SSK, K1, P2, K2, YO, K1, YO, K2, P6, K1, K2 tog †, YO, slip 1 as if to **knit**, K2 tog, PSSO, YO, repeat from † to † once, K1.

Row 12: Repeat Row 8.

Row 14: Repeat Row 6.

Row 16: Repeat Row 4.

Row 18: K1, † SSK, K1, P6, K2, YO, K1, YO, K2, P2, K1, K2 tog †, YO, slip 1 as if to **knit**, K2 tog, PSSO, YO, repeat from † to † once, K1.

Row 20: K1, † SSK, K1, P7, K2, YO, K1, YO, K2, P1, K1, K2 tog †, K3, repeat from † to † once, K1.

Row 22: Repeat Row 18.

Repeat Rows 3-22 for pattern until Scarf measures approximately 49³/₄" (126.5 cm) from cast on edge, ending by working Row 9.

Last Row: K1, † SSK, K1, P2, K2, YO, K1, YO, K2, P6, K1, K2 tog †, P3, repeat from † to † once, K1.

Bind off all sts in **purl**.

Design by Cathy Hardy.

By noon it was apparent that Macy had made substantial progress on the mural. The sketch was completely finished now and she'd started painting. The colors she'd chosen were bright and bold, acrylics rather than oils. The entire office seemed enthralled with her work, judging by all the chatter about what a wonderful job she *was doing.*
—Hannah's List

macy's 3-color PULLOVER

Isn't this a gorgeous sweater that Macy is modeling? As it turns out, these are also nice colors for a redhead to wear. Don't be surprised if you see the same sweater in hot pink and purple go zooming past you on a bicycle someday. Worn by a redhead, of course.

◼◼◼◻ INTERMEDIATE

Size	Finished Chest Measurement	
Extra Small	28¹/₂"	(72.5 cm)
Small	32"	(81.5 cm)
Medium	35"	(89 cm)
Large	38¹/₂"	(98 cm)
Extra Large	41¹/₂"	(105.5 cm)
2X-Large	44¹/₂"	(113 cm)

Size Note: Instructions are written with sizes Extra Small, Small, and Medium in the first set of braces { } and sizes Large, Extra Large, and 2X-Large in the second set of braces. Instructions will be easier to read if you circle all the numbers pertaining to your size. If only one number is given, it applies to all sizes.

MATERIALS

Medium Weight Yarn
[3 ounces, 185 yards
(85 grams, 170 meters) per skein]:
   Color A (Green) - {4-4-5}{5-6-6} skeins
   Color B (Teal) - {1-1-2}{2-2-2} skein(s)
   Color C (Coral) - 1 skein
Straight knitting needles, size 7 (4.5 mm)
  or size needed for gauge
16" (40.5 cm) Circular knitting needle,
  size 6 (4 mm)
Cable needle
Stitch holders - 2
Marker
Yarn needle

Techniques used: • K2 tog *(Fig. 8, page 44)*; w• SSK *(Figs. 9a-c, page 45);* and • increases *(Figs. 7a & b, page 44).*

GAUGE: With larger size needles,
    in Stockinette Stitch,
    20 sts and 24 rows = 4" (10 cm)

STITCH GUIDE

FRONT CABLE (uses 3 sts)
Slip next st onto cable needle and hold in **front** of work, K2 from left needle, K1 from cable needle.
BACK CABLE (uses 3 sts)
Slip next 2 sts onto cable needle and hold in **back** of work, K1 from left needle, K2 from cable needle.

BACK

Using larger size needles and Color B, cast on {74-82-90}{98-106-114} sts.

Rows 1-5: (K1, P1) across.

Instructions continued on page 32.

Macy dressed in white jeans and an olive-green sweater, then ran a brush through her tangle of red curls. The makeup people would see to her hair and face later. This assignment, a photo shoot for a yarn company catalog, was scheduled for eleven. Radio was more fun, but the money she made from modeling put food in the cats' dishes.

—*Hannah's List*

Carry unused color loosely along side of piece.

When instructed to slip a stitch (that is not part of a decrease), always slip as if to **purl** with yarn held **loosely** to **wrong** side.

Row 6 (Right side): Using Color A, K2, (slip 1, K3) across.

Row 7: (P3, slip 1) across to last 2 sts, P2.

Row 8: Using Color B, K4, slip 1, (K3, slip 1) across to last st, K1.

Row 9: P1, slip 1, (P3, slip 1) across to last 4 sts, P4.

Rows 10-25: Repeat Rows 6-9, 4 times.

Cut Color B. Using Color A and beginning with a knit row, work in Stockinette Stitch (knit one row, purl one row) until piece measures approximately {5³/₄-5³/₄-7}{7¹/₄-8¹/₄-7³/₄}"/ {14.5-14.5-18}{18.5-21-19.5} cm from cast on edge, ending by working a **purl** row.

Note: Placement of Stripe can be adjusted to be placed at the waistline.

STRIPE
Row 1: Using Color B, knit across.

Row 2: Purl across.

Row 3: Using Color C, K2, (slip 1, K3) across.

Row 4: (P3, slip 1) across to last 2 sts, P2; cut Color C.

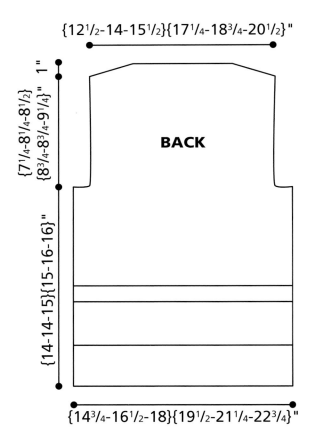

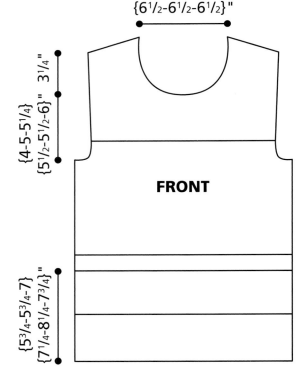

Note: Pieces include two edge stitches.

Row 5: Using Color B, knit across.

Row 6: Purl across.

Cut Color B. Using Color A, work in Stockinette Stitch until piece measures approximately {14-14-15}{15-16-16}"/{35.5-35.5-38}{38-40.5-40.5} cm from cast on edge, ending by working a **purl** row.

ARMHOLE SHAPING
Rows 1 and 2: Bind off 4 sts, work across: {66-74-82}{90-98-106} sts.

Row 3 (Decrease row)**:** K1, SSK, knit across to last 3 sts, K2 tog, K1: {64-72-80}{88-96-104} sts.

Row 4: Purl across.

Row 5: Repeat Row 3: {62-70-78}{86-94-102} sts.

Work even until Armholes measure approximately {7$\frac{1}{4}$-8$\frac{1}{4}$-8$\frac{1}{2}$}{8$\frac{3}{4}$-8$\frac{3}{4}$-9$\frac{1}{4}$}"/{18.5-21-21.5}{22-22-23.5} cm, ending by working a **purl** row.

SHOULDER SHAPING
Rows 1-4: Bind off {6-7-8}{9-10-12} sts, work across: {38-42-46}{50-54-54} sts.

Rows 5 and 6: Bind off {5-6-8}{9-11-11} sts, work across: {28-30-30}{32-32-32} sts.

Slip remaining sts onto st holder; cut yarn.

FRONT
Work same as Back through Row {6-8-6}{8-8-6} of Armhole; do **not** cut Color A: {62-70-78}{86-94-102} sts.

YOKE
Row 1: Using Color C, knit across.

Row 2: Purl across.

Row 3: Using Color A, K2, (slip 1, K3) across.

Row 4: (P3, slip 1) across to last 2 sts, P2.

Row 5: Using Color C, K2, (work Front Cable, K1) across.

Row 6: Purl across.

Row 7: Using Color A, K6, (slip 1, K3) across.

Row 8: (P3, slip 1) across to last 6 sts, P6.

Row 9: Using Color C, K4, work Back Cable, (K1, work Back Cable) across to last 3 sts, K3.

Row 10: Purl across.

Repeat Rows 3-10 for Yoke pattern until Armholes measure approximately {4-5-5$\frac{1}{4}$}{5$\frac{1}{2}$-5$\frac{1}{2}$-6}"/{10-12.5-13.5}{14-14-15} cm, ending by working Row 6 or Row 10.

NECK SHAPING
Both sides of Neck are worked at the same time using separate yarn for **each** side. Maintain established pattern.

Tip: Only slip a stitch in pattern at neck edge if there are enough sts to work the 3-stitch cable on the next Color C row.

Row 1: Work across {20-23-27}{30-34-38} sts; slip next {22-24-24}{26-26-26} sts onto st holder; with second yarn, work across: {20-23-27}{30-34-38} sts **each** side.

Row 2: Work across; with second yarn, work across.

Row 3 (Decrease row)**:** Work across to within 3 sts of neck edge, K2 tog, K1; with second yarn, K1, SSK, work across: {19-22-26}{29-33-37} sts **each** side.

Rows 4-7: Repeat Rows 2 and 3 twice: {17-20-24}{27-31-35} sts **each** side.

Work even until Front measures same as Back to Shoulder Shaping, ending by working Row 6 or Row 10; cut Color C.

Instructions continued on page 34.

SHOULDER SHAPING

Work shaping in Stockinette Stitch using Color A.

Rows 1-4: Bind off {6-7-8}{9-10-12} sts, work across; with second yarn, work across: {5-6-8}{9-11-11} sts **each** side.

Row 5: Bind off remaining sts on first side leaving long end for sewing; with second yarn, work across.

Bind off remaining sts leaving long end for sewing.

SLEEVE
CUFF
Using larger size needles and Color B, cast {38-42-42}{46-46-50} sts.

Work same as Back through Row 25; cut Color B.

BODY
Rows 1-4: Using Color A and beginning with a knit row, work in Stockinette Stitch.

Increases are made by knitting into the front **and** into the back of the next stitch.

Row 5 (Increase row): K1, increase, knit across to last 2 sts, increase, K1: {40-44-44}{48-48-52} sts.

Rows 6-10: Work in Stockinette Stitch.

STRIPE
Row 1 (Increase row)**:** Using Color B, K1, increase, knit across to last 2 sts, increase, K1: {42-46-46}{50-50-54} sts.

Row 2: Purl across.

Row 3: Using Color C, K4, slip 1, (K3, slip 1) across to last st, K1.

Row 4: P1, slip 1, (P3, slip 1) across to last 4 sts, P4; cut Color C.

Row 5: Knit across.

Row 6: Purl across; cut Color B.

Using Color A and working in Stockinette Stitch, increase one stitch at **each** edge in same manner on next row, and then every sixth row, {2-5-8}{4-10-10} times **more**; then increase every eighth row, {5-3-1}{4-0-0} time(s) *(see Zeros, page 43)*: {58-64-66}{68-72-76} sts.

Work even until Sleeve measures approximately {17-17¼-17½}{17¾-18-18¼}"/{43-44-44.5}{45-45.5-46.5} cm from cast on edge, ending by working a **purl** row.

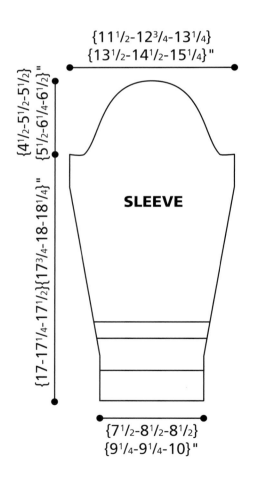

{11½-12¾-13¼}
{13½-14½-15¼}"

{4½-5½-5½}
{5½-6¼-6½}"

{17-17¼-17½}{17¾-18-18¼}"

SLEEVE

{7½-8½-8½}
{9¼-9¼-10}"

SLEEVE CAP

Rows 1 and 2: Bind off 4 sts, work across: {50-56-58}{60-64-68} sts.

Row 3 (Decrease row): K1, SSK, knit across to last 3 sts, K2 tog, K1: {48-54-56}{58-62-66} sts.

Row 4: Purl across.

Rows 5 thru {24-30-30}{30-34-36}: Repeat Rows 3 and 4, {10-13-13}{13-15-16} times: {28-28-30}{32-32-34} sts.

Next 2 Rows: Bind off {4-4-4}{5-5-5} sts, work across: {20-20-22}{22-22-24} sts.

Last 2 Rows: Bind off {4-4-5}{5-5-6} sts, work across: 12 sts.

Bind off remaining sts.

FINISHING

Using long ends, sew shoulder seams.

NECK RIBBING

With **right** side facing, using circular needle and Color B, pick up 24 sts evenly spaced along left Front Neck edge *(Fig. 13a, page 45)*, slip {22-24-24}{26-26-26} sts from Front st holder onto second end of circular needle and knit across, pick up 24 sts evenly spaced along right Front Neck edge, slip {28-30-30}{32-32-32} sts from Back st holder onto second end of circular needle and knit across, place marker to indicate beginning of rnd *(see Markers, page 43)*: {98-102-102}{106-106-106} sts.

Work in K1, P1 ribbing around for 1" (2.5 cm).

Bind off all sts **loosely** in ribbing.

Sew Sleeves to Sweater, placing center of last row on Sleeve Cap at shoulder seam and matching bound off stitches.

Weave underarm and side in one continuous seam *(Fig. 14, page 46)*.

Design by Cathy Hardy.

baby BONNET

This pattern has been in demand lately at A Good Yarn—the knitting shop across the street from Winter's bakery. Winter doesn't knit, but she's noticed that plenty of her regular customers are working on the same bonnet design for Alix's baby. Once the baby arrives, Winter knows she's going to miss working with Alix, who's become a wonderful baker and a close friend.

◼◼☐☐ EASY +

Finished Size: 6 months

MATERIALS

Light Weight Yarn
[1.75 ounces, 161 yards
(50 grams, 147 meters) per skein]:
  1 skein
Straight knitting needles, sizes 5 (3.75 mm)
  and 6 (4 mm) **or** sizes needed for gauge
Cable needle
Tapestry needle
Sewing needle and thread
⅝" (16 mm) Button

Techniques used: • K2 tog *(Fig. 8, page 44)*; • YO *(Fig. 5, page 44)*; and • adding on stitches *(Figs. 6a & b, page 44)*.

GAUGE: With larger size needles,
    in pattern,
    22 sts and 38 rows = 3¾" (9.5 cm)

Gauge Swatch: 3¾" (9.5 cm) square
Using larger size needles, cast on 22 sts.
Row 1: Knit across.
Row 2: K3, P4, K7, P4, K4.
Row 3: K4, work Back Cable, K7, work Back Cable, K3.
Row 4: K3, P4, K7, P4, K4.
Rows 5-38: Repeat Rows 1-4, 8 times; then repeat Rows 1 and 2 once **more**.
Bind off all sts in **knit**.

STITCH GUIDE
BACK CABLE (uses 4 sts)
Slip next 2 sts onto cable needle and hold in **back** of work, K2 from left needle, K2 from cable needle.

CROWN
RIBBING
Using smaller size needles, cast on 75 sts.

Row 1: K1, (P1, K1) across.

Row 2 (Right side): P1, (K1, P1) across.

Repeat Rows 1 and 2 until Ribbing measures approximately 1" (2.5 cm) from cast on edge, ending by working Row 1.

BODY
Change to larger size needles.

Row 1: Knit across.

Row 2: K8, P4, (K7, P4) across to last 8 sts, K8.

Row 3: K8, work Back Cable, (K7, work Back Cable) across to last 8 sts, K8.

Row 4: K8, P4, (K7, P4) across to last 8 sts, K8.

Repeat Rows 1-4 for pattern until Crown measures approximately 5" (12.5 cm) from cast on edge, ending by working Row 4.

Deep in thought, Winter didn't immediately hear Alix knock at the office door. Winter gestured her in. There were only a few weeks left before Alix's due date. Winter was proud of Alix and Jordan, and she envied them, too. Jordan had refinished a used crib and set it up in the baby's room this past weekend. Alix had been knitting for weeks, as had everyone at A Good Yarn, the knitting shop across the street.

—Hannah's List

BACK

Maintain established pattern throughout.

Rows 1 and 2: Bind off 25 sts, work across: 25 sts.

Work even until Back measures approximately 4" (10 cm) from bound off sts, ending by working pattern Row 4.

Bind off all sts in **knit**.

FINISHING

Sew sides of Back to bound off edges of Crown.

NECK RIBBING

With **right** side facing and using smaller size needles, pick up 81 sts across bottom edge *(Figs. 13a & b, page 45)*, **turn**; add on 20 sts: 101 sts.

Row 1: P1, (K1, P1) across.

Row 2: K1, (P1, K1) across.

Row 3: P1, (K1, P1) across.

Row 4: K1, (P1, K1) across.

Row 5 (Buttonhole row)**:** P1, K2 tog, YO, (K1, P1) across.

Rows 6-9: Repeat Rows 2 and 3 twice.

Bind off all sts **loosely** in ribbing.

Sew button on left side of Neck Ribbing.

Design by Lois J. Long.

baby BLANKET

There can't be anything in the world more rewarding to knit than a baby blanket! Lydia Goetz's teenage daughter prefers to crochet, but she's patiently learning to knit a baby blanket for her friend Alix. Casey chose blue yarn, but what if the baby isn't a boy? Maybe Lydia can show her how to knit lace to add to the blanket.

◖■◻◻ EASY

Finished Size: 38½"w x 36"h (98 cm x 91.5 cm)

MATERIALS

Medium Weight Yarn
[3.5 ounces, 170 yards
(100 grams, 156 meters) per skein]:
  6 skeins
24" (61 cm) Circular knitting needles, sizes
  7 (4.5 mm) **and** 8 (5 mm) **or** sizes needed
  for gauge

GAUGE: With larger size needle, in pattern,
  2 repeats (20 sts) = 4¾" (12 cm);
  2 row repeats (24 rows) = 4" (10 cm)

Gauge Swatch: 4¾"w x 4"h (12 cm x 10 cm)
Using larger size needle, cast on 20 sts.
Row 1: Purl across.
Row 2 (Right side): (K2, P8) twice.
Row 3: (K8, P2) twice.
Row 4: (K2, P2, K4, P2) twice.
Row 5: (K2, P4, K2, P2) twice.
Rows 6-9: Repeat Rows 4 and 5 twice.
Rows 10 and 11: Repeat Rows 2 and 3.
Row 12: Knit across.
Rows 13-24: Repeat Rows 1-12.
Bind off all sts in **knit**.

BOTTOM BORDER
Using smaller size needle, cast on 162 sts.

Rows 1-8: Knit across.

BODY
Change to larger size needle.

Row 1: K5, purl across to last 5 sts, K5.

Row 2 (Right side): K7, P8, (K2, P8) across to last 7 sts, K7.

Row 3: K5, P2, (K8, P2) across to last 5 sts, K5.

Row 4: K7, P2, K4, P2, (K2, P2, K4, P2) across to last 7 sts, K7.

Row 5: K5, P2, (K2, P4, K2, P2) across to last 5 sts, K5.

Rows 6-9: Repeat Rows 4 and 5 twice.

Rows 10 and 11: Repeat Rows 2 and 3.

Row 12: Knit across.

Repeat Rows 1-12 for pattern until Blanket measures approximately 35½" (90 cm) from cast on edge, ending by working Row 1.

TOP BORDER
Rows 1-7: Using smaller size needle, knit across.

Bind off all sts in **knit**.

Design by Lois J. Long.

Winter caught the phone just before it went to voice mail.

"Alix is having her baby!" Lydia, from A Good Yarn, shouted. "She called a few minutes ago and she's in labor."

Winter was excited when they arrived at the hospital. To her surprise she discovered the waiting room was full. Alix's in-laws were sitting across from Lydia Goetz and Casey, her thirteen-year-old daughter. Winter could see that Casey had brought her knitting.

Casey said, "I'm knitting the baby a blanket. Mom's helping me."

—Hannah's List

thank you for helping
WARM UP america!

Since 1991, Warm Up America! has donated more than 250,000 afghans to battered women's shelters, victims of natural disasters, the homeless, and many others who are in need.

You can help Warm Up America! help others, and with so little effort. Debbie urges everyone who uses the patterns in this book to take a few minutes to work a 7" x 9" block for this worthy cause. To help you get started, she's providing these two block patterns.

If you are able to provide a completed afghan, Warm Up America! requests that you donate it directly to any charity or social services agency in your community. If you require assistance in assembling the blocks into an afghan, please include your name and address inside the packaging and ship your 7" x 9" blocks to:

Warm Up America! Foundation
2500 Lowell Road
Ranlo, NC 28054

Remember, just a little bit of yarn can make a big difference to someone in need!

Basic patchwork afghans are made of forty-nine 7" x 9" (18 cm x 23 cm) rectangular blocks that are sewn together. Any pattern stitch can be used for the rectangle. Use acrylic medium weight yarn and size 8 (5 mm) straight knitting needles or size needed to obtain the gauge of 9 stitches to 2" (5 cm).

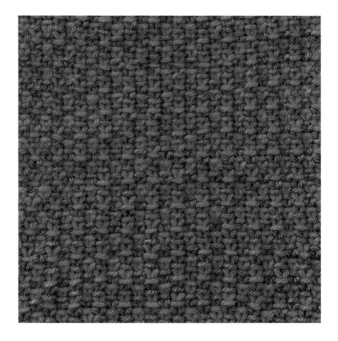

TWISTED SEED BLOCK
Multiple of 2 sts + 1.

Cast on 31 sts.

Row 1: P1, (K1, P1) across.

Row 2 (Right side)**:** K1, (K1 tbl, K1) across *(Fig. 3, page 44)*.

Row 3: P2, K1, (P1, K1) across to last 2 sts, P2.

Row 4: K2, K1 tbl, (K1, K1 tbl) across to last 2 sts, K2.

Repeat Rows 1-4 for pattern until Block measures approximately 9" (23 cm) from cast on edge, ending by working a **wrong** side row.

Bind off all sts in pattern.

2-COLOR WOVEN BLOCK
Multiple of 2 sts + 1.

You will need two colors.

Using Color A, cast on 31 sts.

When instructed to slip a stitch, always slip as if to **purl** with yarn held **loosely** to **right** side so that the carried strand shows on the right side forming the woven look.

Row 1 (Right side)**:** K1, (slip 1, K1) across.

Row 2: P2, slip 1, (P1, slip 1) across to last 2 sts, P2.

Repeat Rows 1 and 2 changing colors every 2 rows, and carrying unused yarn loosely along side of piece, until Block measures approximately 9" (23 cm) from cast on edge, ending by working a **right** side row.

Bind off all sts in **purl**.

ASSEMBLY
Sew Blocks together, forming 7 vertical strips of 7 Blocks each and measuring 7" x 63" (18 cm x 160 cm). Sew strips together.

ABBREVIATIONS

cm	centimeters
K	knit
mm	millimeters
P	purl
PSSO	pass slipped stitch over
Rnd(s)	round(s)
SSK	slip, slip, knit
SSP	slip, slip, purl
st(s)	stitch(es)
tbl	through back loop
tog	together
YO	yarn over

★ — work instructions following ★ as many **more** times as indicated in addition to the first time.

† to † — work all instructions from first † to second † as **many** times as specified.

( ) or [ ] — work enclosed instructions **as many** times as specified by the number immediately following **or** contains explanatory remarks.

colon (:) — the number given after a colon at the end of a row or round denotes the number of stitches you should have on that row or round.

work even — work without increasing or decreasing in the established pattern.

KNIT TERMINOLOGY	
UNITED STATES	**INTERNATIONAL**
gauge =	tension
bind off =	cast off
yarn over (YO) =	yarn forward (yfwd) **or** yarn around needle (yrn)

Yarn Weight Symbol & Names	LACE 0	SUPER FINE 1	FINE 2	LIGHT 3	MEDIUM 4	BULKY 5	SUPER BULKY 6
Type of Yarns in Category	Fingering, size 10 crochet thread	Sock, Fingering, Baby	Sport, Baby	DK, Light Worsted	Worsted, Afghan, Aran	Chunky, Craft, Rug	Bulky, Roving
Knit Gauge Range* in Stockinette St to 4" (10 cm)	33-40** sts	27-32 sts	23-26 sts	21-24 sts	16-20 sts	12-15 sts	6-11 sts
Advised Needle Size Range	000-1	1 to 3	3 to 5	5 to 7	7 to 9	9 to 11	11 and larger

*GUIDELINES ONLY: The chart above reflects the most commonly used gauges and needle sizes for specific yarn categories.

** Lace weight yarns are usually knitted on larger needles to create lacy openwork patterns. Accordingly, a gauge range is difficult to determine. Always follow the gauge stated in your pattern.

KNITTING NEEDLES																
U.S.	0	1	2	3	4	5	6	7	8	9	10	10½	11	13	15	17
U.K.	13	12	11	10	9	8	7	6	5	4	3	2	1	00	000	---
Metric - mm	2	2.25	2.75	3.25	3.5	3.75	4	4.5	5	5.5	6	6.5	8	9	10	12.75

■□□□ BEGINNER	Projects for first-time knitters using basic knit and purl stitches. Minimal shaping.
■■□□ EASY	Projects using basic stitches, repetitive stitch patterns, simple color changes, and simple shaping and finishing.
■■■□ INTERMEDIATE	Projects with a variety of stitches, such as basic cables and lace, simple intarsia, double-pointed needles and knitting in the round needle techniques, mid-level shaping and finishing.
■■■■ EXPERIENCED	Projects using advanced techniques and stitches, such as short rows, fair isle, more intricate intarsia, cables, lace patterns, and numerous color changes.

GAUGE

Exact gauge is **essential** for proper size. Before beginning your project, make a sample swatch in the yarn and needle specified in the individual instructions. After completing the swatch, measure it, counting your stitches and rows or rounds carefully. If your swatch is larger or smaller than specified, **make another, changing needle size to get the correct gauge**. Keep trying until you find the size needles that will give you the specified gauge. Once proper gauge is obtained, measure width approximately every 3" (7.5 cm) to be sure gauge remains consistent.

ZEROS

To consolidate the length of an involved pattern, zeros are sometimes used so that all sizes can be combined. For example, decrease every fourth row, {5-4-0} times means that the first size would decrease 5 times, the second size would decrease 4 times, and the largest size would do nothing.

DOUBLE POINTED NEEDLES

The stitches are divided evenly between four double pointed needles as specified in the individual pattern. Form a square with the four needles *(Fig. 1)*. Do **not** twist the cast on ridge. With the remaining needle, work across the stitches on the first needle. You will now have an empty needle with which to work the stitches from the next needle. Work the first stitch of each needle firmly to prevent gaps. Continue working around without turning the work.

Fig. 1

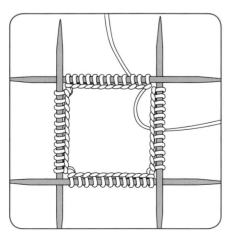

USING CIRCULAR NEEDLE

Using a circular needle, cast on all stitches as instructed. Untwist and straighten the stitches on the needle to be sure that the cast on ridge lays on the inside of the needle and never rolls around the needle.

Hold the needle so that the ball of yarn is attached to the stitch closest to the **right** hand point. Working each round on the outside of the circle, with the **right** side of the knitting facing you, work across the stitches on the left hand point *(Fig. 2)*.

Check to be sure that the cast on edge has not twisted around the needle. If it has, it is impossible to untwist it. The only way to fix this is to rip it out and return to the cast on row.

Fig. 2

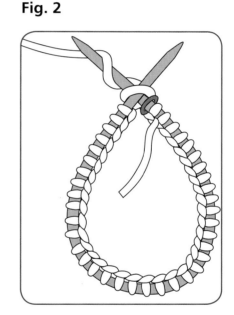

MARKERS

As a convenience to you, we have used markers to mark the beginning of a round and to mark placement of decreases. Place markers as instructed. You may use purchased markers or tie a length of contrasting color yarn around the needle. When you reach a marker, slip it from the left needle to the right needle; remove it when no longer needed. When using double pointed needles, a split-ring marker can be placed around the first stitch in the round to indicate the beginning of the round. Move it up at the end of each round.

KNIT ONE THROUGH BACK LOOP
(abbreviated K1 tbl)
Insert the right needle into the **back** of the next stitch from **front** to **back** *(Fig. 3)* and **knit** the stitch.

Fig. 3

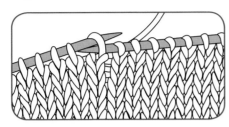

CHANGING COLORS
When changing colors, always pick up the new color yarn from beneath the dropped yarn and keep the color which has just been worked to the left *(Fig. 4)*. This will prevent holes in the finished piece. Take extra care to keep your tension even.

Fig. 4

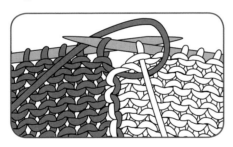

YARN OVER *(abbreviated YO)*
Bring the yarn forward **between** the needles, then back **over** the top of the right hand needle, so that it is now in position to knit the next stitch *(Fig. 5)*.

Fig. 5

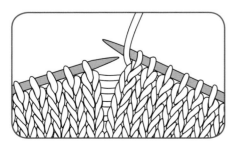

ADDING NEW STITCHES
Insert the right needle into the stitch as if to **knit**, yarn over and pull the loop through *(Fig. 6a)*, insert the left needle into the loop just worked from **front** to **back** and slip the loop onto the left needle *(Fig. 6b)*. Repeat for required number of stitches.

Fig. 6a   **Fig. 6b**

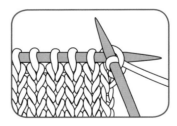   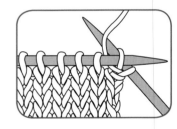

INCREASE
Knit the next stitch but do **not** slip the old stitch off the left needle *(Fig. 7a)*. Insert the right needle into the **back** loop of the **same** stitch and knit it *(Fig. 7b)*, then slip the old stitch off the left needle.

Fig. 7a   **Fig. 7b**

DECREASES
KNIT 2 TOGETHER *(abbreviated K2 tog)*
Insert the right needle into the **front** of the first two stitches on the left needle as if to **knit** *(Fig. 8)*, then **knit** them together as if they were one stitch.

Fig. 8

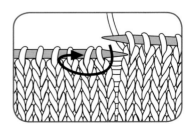

SLIP, SLIP, KNIT *(abbreviated SSK)*

Slip the first stitch as if to **knit**, then slip the next stitch as if to **knit** *(Fig. 9a)*. Insert the **left** needle into the **front** of both slipped stitches *(Fig. 9b)* and knit them together as if they were one stitch *(Fig. 9c)*.

Fig. 9a

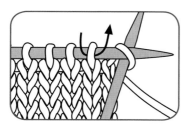

Fig. 9b

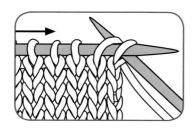

Fig. 9c

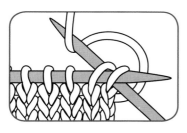

SLIP 1, KNIT 2 TOGETHER, PASS SLIPPED STITCH OVER
(abbreviated slip 1, K2 tog, PSSO)

Slip one stitch as if to **knit**. Knit the next two stitches together *(Fig. 8, page 44)*. With the left needle, bring the slipped stitch over the stitch just made *(Fig. 10)* and off the needle.

Fig. 10

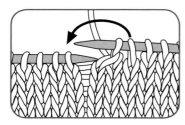

PURL 2 TOGETHER *(abbreviated P2 tog)*

Insert the right needle into the **front** of the first two stitches on the left needle as if to **purl** *(Fig. 11)*, then **purl** them together as if they were one stitch.

Fig. 11

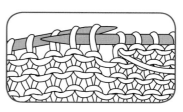

SLIP, SLIP, PURL *(abbreviated SSP)*

Slip the first stitch as if to **knit**, then slip the next stitch as if to **knit** *(Fig. 9a)*. Place these two stitches back onto the left needle. Insert the **right** needle into the **back** of both slipped stitches from the **back** to **front** *(Fig. 12)* and purl them together as if they were one stitch.

Fig. 12

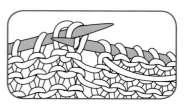

PICKING UP STITCHES

When instructed to pick up stitches, insert the needle from the **front** to the **back** under two strands at the edge of the worked piece *(Fig. 13a or b)*. Put the yarn around the needle as if to **knit**, then bring the needle with the yarn back through the stitch to the right side, resulting in a stitch on the needle.

Repeat this along the edge, picking up the required number of stitches.

A crochet hook may be helpful to pull yarn through.

Fig. 13a

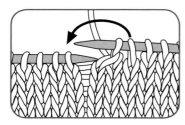

Fig. 13b

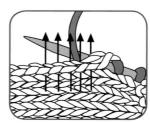

WEAVING SEAMS

With the **right** side of both pieces facing you and edges even, sew through both pieces once to secure the beginning of the seam, leaving an ample yarn end to weave in later. Insert the needle under the bar **between** the first and second stitches on the row and pull the yarn through *(Fig. 14)*. Insert the needle under the next bar on the second side. Repeat from side to side, being careful to match rows. If the edges are different lengths, it may be necessary to insert the needle under two bars at one edge.

Fig. 14

GRAFTING

Thread the yarn needle with the long end. Hold the threaded yarn needle on the right side of work. Work in the following sequence, pulling yarn through as if to knit or as if to purl with even tension and keeping yarn under points of needles to avoid tangling and extra loops.

Step 1: Purl first stitch on **front** needle, leave on *(Fig. 15a)*.
Step 2: Knit first stitch on **back** needle, leave on *(Fig. 15b)*.
Step 3: Knit first stitch on **front** needle, slip off.
Step 4: Purl next stitch on **front** needle, leave on.
Step 5: Purl first stitch on **back** needle, slip off.
Step 6: Knit next stitch on **back** needle, leave on.
Repeat Steps 3-6 across until all stitches are worked off the needles.

Fig. 15a   **Fig. 15b**

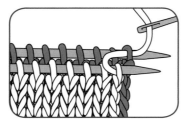

3-NEEDLE BIND OFF

Holding pieces with **right** sides together and needles parallel to each other, insert a third needle as if to **knit** into the first stitch on the front needle **and** into the first stitch on the back needle *(Fig. 16)*. Knit these two stitches together and slip them off the needle. ★ Knit the next stitch on each needle together and slip them off the needle. To bind off, insert one of the left needles into the first stitch on the right needle and bring the first stitch over the second stitch and off the right needle; repeat from ★ across until all of the stitches have been bound off.

Fig. 16

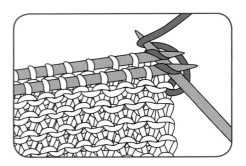

BLOCKING

Place the item to be blocked on a clean terry towel over a flat surface and shape; pin in place using rust-proof pins where needed. Hold a steam iron or steamer just above the item and steam it thoroughly. Never let the weight of the iron touch the item because it will flatten the stitches. Leave the item pinned until it is completely dry.

INFORMATION

The projects in this book were made using a variety of yarns. Any brand in the specified weight may be used. It is best to refer to the yardage/meters when determining how many skeins or hanks to purchase. Remember, to arrive at the finished size, it is the GAUGE/TENSION that is important, not the brand of yarn.
For your convenience, listed below are the specific yarns used to create our photography models.

LACE SHAWL
Cascade Yarns, "Cloud 9"
#176 (Lt Blue)

SAMMY'S DOG SWEATER
Red Heart® Classic™
Teal - #0683 Lt Seafoam
Red Heart® Super Saver®
Brown - #0360 Café

CAT'S BUTTERFLY
Coats® Crème de la Crème™
Main Color - #0205 Golden Yellow
Main Color - #0935 Taffy Stripe Ombre
Black - #0012 Black

SCULPTURED PILLOWS
Cascade Yarns, 220 Heathers
#2437 (Tan)

AFGHAN
Patons® Décor
#87309 New Lilac

HARVEY'S VEST
Patons® Classic Wool
#00208 Burgundy

HARVEY'S CREW SOCKS
Patons® Kroy Socks
#55012 Glencheck

HANNAH'S ANKLE SOCKS
Red Heart® Heart & Sole™
Main Color - #3970 Faded Jeans
Contrasting Color - #3115 Ivory

STYLISH SCARF
Cascade Yarns, Venezia Worsted
#108 (Orange)

MACY'S 3-COLOR PULLOVER
Caron® Country
Color A - #0012 Foliage
Color B - #0021 Peacock
Color C - #0010 Sunset

BABY BONNET
Patons® Astra
#02943 Maize Yellow

BABY BLANKET
Lion Brand® Vanna's Choice® Baby
#106 Little Boy Blue

WARM UP AMERICA BLOCKS
Lion Brand® Vanna's Choice®
#124 Toffee
#134 Terracotta

Instructions tested and photo models made by JoAnn Bowling, Lee Ellis, Sue Galucki, Raymelle Greening, Dale Potter, Margaret Taverner, and Ted Tomany.